Fact Finders®

The Story of the
American Revolution

The U.S. Constitution, Bill of Rights, and a New Nation

by Steven Otfinoski

Consultant:
Philip Bigler
Former Director, The James Madison Center
Harrisonburg, Virginia

CAPSTONE PRESS
a capstone imprint

Fact Finders are published by Capstone Press,
1710 Roe Crest Drive, North Mankato, Minnesota 56003.
www.capstonepub.com

Library of Congress Cataloging-in-Publication Data
Otfinoski, Steven.
The U.S. Constitution, Bill of Rights, and a new nation / by Steven Otfinoski.
p. cm.—(Fact finders. The story of the American Revolution)
Includes bibliographical references and index.
Summary: "Describes the outcome of the Revolutionary War, including the U.S.
     Constitution and the Bill of Rights"—Provided by publisher.
 ISBN 978-1-4296-8589-4 (library binding)
 ISBN 978-1-4296-9292-2 (paperback)
 ISBN 978-1-62065-248-0 (eBook PDF)
1. United States. Constitution—Juvenile literature. 2. Constitutional history
United States—Juvenile literature. 3. United States—Politics and
government—1775–1783—Juvenile literature. 4. United States—Politics
and government—1783–1789—Juvenile literature. I. Title.
E303.O85 2013
342.7302'9—dc23   2012011885

Editorial Credits
Jennifer Besel and Lori Shores, editors; Heidi Thompson and Kyle Grenz, designers;
     Wanda Winch, media researcher; Jennifer Walker, production specialist

Photo Credits
Alamy: Everett Collection Inc., 9, 28, North Wind Picture Archives, 4, 11, 12, 15,
18, 22; Architect of the Capitol, 17; Capstone: cover, 29 (map); Corbis: Bettmann,
10, 19, 23; Library of Congress: Prints and Photographs Division, 6, 7, 8, 13, 14,
24, 25, 26 (bottom); Louis S. Glanzman, 20; National Parks Service: Colonial
National Historical Park/Keith Rocco, artist, 5; North Wind Picture Archives, 21;
Shutterstock: Christophe Boisson, grunge stripe background, Mike Flippo, 26
(top), Perry Correll, 29 (flag)

Printed in the United States of America in Brainerd, Minnesota.
032012   006672BANGF12

Table of Contents

Direct quotations appear on the following pages:

Page 5, from *The Ideological Origins of the American Revolution* by Bernard Baylin (Cambridge, Mass.: The Belknap Press of Harvard University Press, 1992.)

Page 15, from *The Constitutional Convention of 1787 : A Comprehensive Encyclopedia of America's Founding* by John R. Vile (Santa Barbara, Calif.: ABC-CLIO, 2005.)

Page 25, from "One Cent," *Jackson Sentinel*, December 21, 1876, http://newspaperarchive.com/jackson-sentinel/1876-12-21/page-5

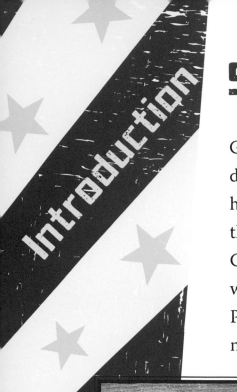

Surrender!

In October 1781, British commander General Charles Cornwallis faced a difficult decision. For three weeks Cornwallis' army had been fighting the Continental army and their French allies at Yorktown, Virginia. Cornwallis' army was under siege. They were outnumbered and losing. When the Patriots overtook his army, Cornwallis had no choice but to surrender.

Patriot forces overwhelmed the British at Yorktown with more than twice as many troops.

siege: an attack designed to surround a place and cut it off from supplies or help

> "The American war is over; but this is far from being the case with the American Revolution. On the contrary, nothing but the first act of the drama is closed."
> Dr. Benjamin Rush, colonial leader from Pennsylvania

The Patriots had been fighting for their independence from Britain for five years. With the surrender at Yorktown, the war was over. But the revolution wasn't. Fighting in some areas continued for more than a year. When peace did come, the new nation faced many problems. The struggle to create a nation was far from finished.

The Surrender at Yorktown took place on October 19, 1781.

CHAPTER 1

War Ends

In September 1783, American and British leaders met in France. There they signed the Treaty of Paris, officially ending the war. However, this move did not settle all issues for the new nation. In the treaty, Britain recognized the United States as an independent nation. In return, the states would be urged to pay money owed to Britain from before the war. But the U.S. government couldn't force the states to do so, and most debts went unpaid. Patriots had taken Loyalist property during the war. Under the treaty, the U.S. government agreed to return or pay for the property. But few Loyalists received their property or payment.

John Jay, Benjamin Franklin (both standing, left) and John Adams (seated, middle) worked on the Treaty of Paris with British officials.

Loyalist: a colonist who was loyal to Great Britain during the Revolutionary War

FAST FACTS

About 20,000 Loyalists fought with the British III the war. Their numbers, at times, were greater than all the soldiers in Washington's army.

Weeks after the British surrender, General George Washington entered New York to a crowd of cheering Patriots.

Americans celebrated their independence. But joy quickly turned to questions. The nation faced an uncertain future. The United States owed about $12 million to other countries for wartime supplies and weapons. States owed another $25 million to citizens who had provided food and supplies to the army. Money and jobs were hard to find. Could the United States survive? No one knew.

CHAPTER 2

A Weak Government

Under the Articles of Confederation, states supported one another during the war. The Articles created a government with a president of Congress, but no chief executive. It also had no court system. Only Congress could pass laws for the nation. Each state was represented in Congress but had only one vote in creating laws. Nine of the 13 states had to vote in favor of passing a new law.

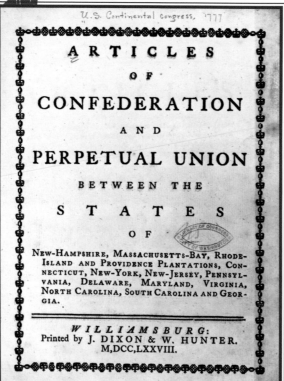

U.S. Continental Congress, 1777

ARTICLES

OF

CONFEDERATION

AND

PERPETUAL UNION

BETWEEN THE

STATES

OF

NEW-HAMPSHIRE, MASSACHUSETTS-BAY, RHODE-ISLAND AND PROVIDENCE PLANTATIONS, CONNECTICUT, NEW-YORK, NEW-JERSEY, PENNSYLVANIA, DELAWARE, MARYLAND, VIRGINIA, NORTH CAROLINA, SOUTH CAROLINA AND GEORGIA.

WILLIAMSBURG:
Printed by J. DIXON & W. HUNTER.
M,DCC,LXXVIII.

confederation: a group that works together and shares leadership

States had the most power under the Articles of Confederation. Congress could declare war and make agreements with other countries. But the government couldn't raise an army, control trade, or collect taxes. State governments collected taxes and had other powers within each state.

At the end of the war, the New York City Hall served as the Capitol of the United States.

Americans in Trouble

Farmers were among the Americans most hurt by the new government. With war over, much of the trade in weapons and supplies ended. Farmers couldn't sell extra crops grown for the army. Prices for other goods climbed and many farmers fell into debt. Without money, farmers couldn't pay taxes. State debt collectors took farmers' land to pay off the debts. Farmers who lost their land wanted to change the laws. But in some states, only property owners could vote. Many farmers did not have a say in the laws that affected them.

Shays' Rebellion

Frustration was greatest in Massachusetts. Led by Revolutionary War veteran Daniel Shays, farmers took up arms against the government. Massachusetts asked Congress for help. But under the Articles of Confederation, Congress could not raise an army.

Outside of courthouses, people protested the taking of land and possessions from struggling farmers.

In 1786 Shays marched into Springfield, Massachussets with an army of men. Their goal was to demand that the government lower taxes. They also wanted to stop debt trials and the taking of property. But Shays' men met a local army that drove them out. Shays returned again to Springfield with 1,200 men. The armies clashed and shots were fired. The rebels scattered, and Shays fled to Vermont.

Loyalists and Indians

In April 1783, 7,000 Loyalists sailed for Britain from New York. They were the last of about 100,000 Loyalists to leave America for Canada, Britain, or the West Indies. Patriots rejected Loyalists for not supporting the fight for freedom. In time, however, Loyalists who stayed were accepted back into society.

American Indians also had a difficult time after the war. Tribes had fought for both sides during the war. By doing so, they hoped the winner would return lands taken from them. But neither side acknowledged their help.

A local army attacked protesters during Shays' Rebellion.

Shays' Rebellion didn't turn out as well as people had hoped. It did, however, force lawmakers to make changes. Taxes and court costs were decreased. Shays' Rebellion also influenced Americans by showing the weaknesses of the federal government. People feared that more rebellions would happen in other states. Some people thought the only way to maintain law and order was to create a strong central government.

FAST FACTS

The post-war government was too weak to protect American interests. The weakness prevented the government from solving economic problems, including providing pay to veterans.

Trade between states was also difficult. In September 1786, delegates from five states met in Annapolis, Maryland, to improve trade rules. Many states were not represented. Some states felt it wasn't important. Other state delegates arrived too late to participate. Too few delegates took part to accomplish anything. Alexander Hamilton and James Madison suggested meeting again in Philadelphia the following May to solve growing problems. The delegates agreed to attend the next convention to amend the Articles of Confederation.

Alexander Hamilton helped organize the Constitutional Convention in Philadelphia.

delegate: someone who represents other people at a meeting or in government

amend: to change a law or legal document

CHAPTER 3

A New Constitution

In May 1787, states sent delegates to the meeting, now known as the Constitutional Convention. Muddy roads made travel difficult, and delegates arrived slowly. Finally, the convention began with 29 delegates. By the end, a total of 55 delegates from 12 states had attended. Rhode Island's government disagreed with revising the Articles of Confederation and refused to participate.

After electing George Washington as the convention's president, delegates set rules. First they agreed that issues could be brought up more than once for discussion. They also agreed that discussions should be kept strictly secret. This way the men could freely share their opinions in debate.

George Washington was chosen as convention president because of his achievements during the Revolutionary War.

convention: a large gathering of people who have common interests

The delegates quickly agreed that the Articles of Confederation were too flawed to fix. Instead, they decided to create a new government with a constitution. Some delegates disagreed. They thought the government didn't need to be completely changed, only improved.

"We are razing the foundations of the building, when we need only repair the roof."
-Oliver Ellsworth, delegate from Connecticut

As president of the convention, Washington supervised the debates.

constitution: the written system of laws in a country that state the rights of people and the powers of government

Two Plans

Many delegates shared ideas for the new government. Governor Edmund Randolph of Virginia introduced a plan for a government with legislative, executive, and judicial branches. Congress would make up the legislative branch. This law-making branch would have two parts called the House of Representatives and the Senate. State population would determine the number of members from each state in both parts. Delegates from small states objected to this plan. They thought it was unfair for small states to have less power.

William Paterson of New Jersey came up with another plan. Each state would have the same number of people in both houses. State population wouldn't control how many people served in the houses. Delegates from large states rejected the New Jersey Plan.

The debates continued. The men had heated discussions about how to form the new government. Some delegates became frustrated and left the convention.

Gouverneur Morris is believed to have written the final version of the Constitution.

At least 34 of the delegates were lawyers.

The Constitutional Convention

Despite hot temperatures, windows were kept shut so no one passing by could hear discussions taking place inside.

George Washington didn't participate in the debates, but his character and leadership in the war influenced the group

Benjamin Franklin was ill during the convention. He was often carried into meetings on a chair.

James Madison was the only delegate to attend every meeting. He took detailed notes that were not published until after his death.

Delegates followed strict rules of secrecy. No information was published about the debates as they were held.

The Connecticut Compromise

Debate between the men raged on. Then, on July 11, Roger Sherman presented a third plan. This plan came to be called the Great Compromise because it blended the previous two plans. Sherman suggested that the Senate have two members from every state. Population would determine the number of members in the House of Representatives. Power would be balanced between large and small states. Two weeks later, the delegates voted in favor of the new plan. The Constitution was beginning to take shape.

Roger Sherman was a state delegate for Connecticut.

compromise: a settlement in which each side gives up part of its demands and agrees to the final product

Presidential Power

Next, delegates discussed who would lead the executive branch. Some thought a group of delegates should be elected to lead the executive branch. Most delegates, however, wanted one president in charge. Hamilton recommended that the president be appointed for life. But several delegates thought a life-long president was too similar to a king. Delegates agreed that a president would be elected to a term of four years.

Leaders of the Constitutional Convention

Some of America's best and brightest minds attended the convention. Among them was Gouverneur Morris of New York. He made more speeches at the convention than any other delegate. At age 81, Benjamin Franklin of Philadelphia was the oldest delegate. James Madison spoke in favor of a strong, national government. Madison kept a journal of each meeting. This journal is an important source of information about the convention. Madison, who became known as "The Father of the Constitution," later became America's fourth president.

Elder statesman Benjamin Franklin had a great influence on the Constitutional Convention.

The Constitutional Convention lasted about three months. Not all delegates were able to attend every meeting.

The delegates were creating a republic. This form of government allows citizens to elect representatives for government. But the delegates decided that the public would not be informed well enough to decide on a president. Instead, a group of people who formed an electoral college would elect the president. Electors would be appointed based on the number of delegates each state had in Congress. Electors would then vote for the president as representatives of their states.

The Issue of Slavery

Slavery was not directly mentioned in the Constitution. But it was on the delegates' minds. Northern states wanted to end slavery. Southern states needed slaves to work fields and refused to end slavery. To keep the states united, delegates agreed to compromise. Southern states agreed to ban the international slave trade. They also agreed that slaves could be counted for tax purposes. In return, they could count each slave as "three-fifths of a person" for population purposes. This agreement gave the South more representation in Congress. On January 1, 1808, no more slaves were allowed into the country. Yet slavery continued in the South. Most northerners continued to disagree with slavery. This conflict would eventually lead to America's Civil War.

In 1808 the United States officially banned the buying of slaves from other parts of the world.

FAST FACTS

Gouverneur Morris didn't like the opening phrase "We the people of the States . . ." and suggested "We the people of the United States . . ." It became the document's most famous phrase.

"We The People"

The delegates had decided how the government would run. Next they needed a document that spelled it all out. A committee was formed to write the Constitution. The finished Constitution was only about 4,500 words long. It set up a strong federal government that shared power with the states. The power was balanced among the three branches. A system of checks and balances made sure that no branch would have too much power.

Of the 42 delegates who attended most of the meetings, only 39 signed the Constitution.

The delegates signed the official copy of the Constitution on September 17, 1787. Several delegates were unavailable to sign the document. Some of these delegates favored the Constitution. But some delegates refused to sign because the Constitution did not have a Bill of Rights to protect the rights of citizens.

The Constitution was signed by only 39 of the 55 delegates. However, it was considered unanimous because all delegates who were present signed it.

Constitution supporters agreed to add a Bill of Rights only after the Constitution was agreed on. Once nine states agreed, the Constitution would become law. But there was no guarantee that states would agree to the new government.

CHAPTER 4

The Road to Approval

The road to approval was not smooth. For some states the decision to approve came quickly. Tiny Delaware became the first state to ratify the Constitution. In New York and Virginia, many powerful people opposed the Constitution. Debate in these states was long and heated.

The Federalist Papers

Constitution supporters took their message to the people. Alexander Hamilton, James Madison, and John Jay wrote 85 newspaper essays in favor of the Constitution. They kept their identities secret. The men argued that the Constitution would create a peaceful union of states. This union, they said, would support the welfare of all the states. The essays were popular and helped convince people to accept the Constitution. The essays were published in book form as *The Federalist* in 1788. They later became known as the Federalist Papers.

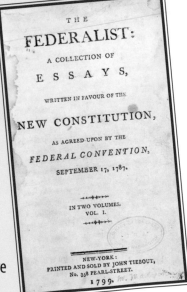

THE
FEDERALIST:
A COLLECTION OF
ESSAYS,
WRITTEN IN FAVOUR OF THE
NEW CONSTITUTION,
AS AGREED-UPON BY THE
FEDERAL CONVENTION,
SEPTEMBER 17, 1787.

IN TWO VOLUMES.
VOL. I.

NEW-YORK:
PRINTED AND SOLD BY JOHN TIEBOUT,
No. 358 PEARL-STREET.
1799.

ratify: to agree or approve officially

"I would rather have a King, a House of Lords and Commons than the new government."
-Patrick Henry, leader of the Anti-Federalists in Virginia

Federalists vs. Anti-Federalists

Debate over the Constitution centered around two groups. Supporters of the Constitution called themselves Federalists. Those who opposed it were Anti-Federalists. These people feared that a central government would

take rights away from the states. They also believed the United States was too big to be governed from one place. The two sides argued in newspapers and pamphlets. The Federalists were better organized. They spread their argument more clearly to the public and other lawmakers.

John Jay did not attend the Constitutional Convention, but he supported the Constitution.

the U.S. Constitution

The Bill of Rights

The Federalists were winning the fight. By May 1789, 11 of 13 states had ratified the Constitution. Still, people worried that individual rights were not protected. Some delegates voted to approve the document because they believed a Bill of Rights would be added to protect people's freedoms.

Later that month the new U.S. Congress met for the first time. James Madison wrote amendments to protect citizens' rights from government power. Congress approved 12 of these amendments. Ten were approved by the states. Together the 10 amendments became known as the Bill of Rights.

James Madison is also known as the "Father of the Bill of Rights."

The Bill of Rights

Amendment	Gives the right to ...
First	... practice religion, speak freely, assemble, address the government, and publish writings.
Second	... own and use guns.
Third	... deny housing to soldiers in time of peace and limit this practice in time of war.
Fourth	... refuse unreasonable searches and seizures of property without a warrant or good reason.
Fifth	... avoid being held for a crime unless they are properly charged; to not be tried twice for the same crime; and to not be forced to testify against yourself.
Sixth	... a speedy trial and a fair jury; to face witnesses; and to have a lawyer when accused of a crime.
Seventh	... a jury trial in federal civil court cases.
Eighth	... fair punishment and fines for crimes.
Ninth	... know that other rights may exist, and they cannot be violated.
Tenth	... assign to the states any power not granted to the federal government

Electing a President

The Constitution was finally approved. It was time to put it into action. The first presidential election took place in 1789. Of the 69 electors who voted, every one cast a ballot for George Washington, who became the president. John Adams had the second highest number of votes and so became the first vice president. On April 30, 1789, Washington took office as the first president of the United States.

George Washington served as president from 1789 to 1797.

The 13 colonies that won their freedom were becoming a strong nation. The American Revolution united the states into one country under one government. It formed a union committed to individual freedoms and a new republican government. The United States was on its way to becoming an independent and powerful nation.

(part of Massachusetts)

N.H.

New York

Mass.

Conn.

Rhode Island

Pennsylvania

New Jersey

Maryland

Delaware

Virginia

Proclamation line of 1763

North Carolina

South Carolina

Georgia

Glossary

amend (uh-MEND)—to change a law or legal document

compromise (KAHM-pruh-myz)—a settlement in which each side gives up part of its demands and agrees to the final product

confederation (kuhn-fed-uh-REY-shun)—a group that works together and shares leadership

constitution (kahn-stuh-TOO-shuhn)—the written system of laws in a country that state the rights of people and the powers of government

convention (kuhn-VEN-shuhn)—a large gathering of people who have common interests

delegate (DEL-uh-guht)—someone who represents other people at a meeting or in government

Loyalist (LOI-uh-list)—a colonist who was loyal to Great Britain during the Revolutionary War

ratify (RAT-uh-fye)—to agree or approve officially

siege (SEEJ)—an attack designed to surround a place and cut it off from supplies or help

Read More

Leavitt, Amie Jane. *The Bill of Rights in Translation: What It Really Means.* Kids' Translations. Mankato, Minn.: Capstone Press, 2009.

Sobel, Syl. *The U.S. Constitution and You.* Hauppauge, N.Y.: Barron's Educational Series, 2012.

Sonneborn, Liz. *The United States Constitution.* Documenting U.S. History. Chicago: Heinemann Library, 2013.

Internet Sites

FactHound offers a safe, fun way to find Internet sites related to this book. All of the sites on FactHound have been researched by our staff.

Here's all you do:

Visit *www.facthound.com*

Type in this code: 9781429685894

Check out projects, games and lots more at
www.capstonekids.com

Index